To:

Beverly

From:

Corinne

Date:

4/18/11

Such a
Wonderful You

Illustrations and text by
Chris Shea

HARVEST HOUSE PUBLISHERS

EUGENE, OREGON

Such a Wonderful You

Copyright © 2010 by Chris Shea
Lifesighs Cards, PO Box 19446, San Diego, CA 92159

Published by Harvest House Publishers
Eugene, Oregon 97402
www.harvesthousepublishers.com

ISBN 978-0-7369-2712-3

Printed in China
10 11 12 13 14 15 16 /LP-NI / 10 9 8 7 6 5 4 3 2

For Lori,
for the elevated thought
of a girl
standing on a
soapbox.

Imagine a day

when one by one

we all took the stage

and shared with each other

things too seldom said,

Words we don't say enough,

verbal little life preservers
that buoy us up and
keep us afloat

on the sometimes
choppy seas of life,

Seas we all sail in the same little boat.

Words like,

I'm sorry, please forgive me...

How can I ever repay you

for everything you've done?

Things like,

Thank you so much...

I appreciate you,

and I know how hard you work.

Imagine a day

when one by one

we all took a pen and
a fresh sheet of paper

and put down
in writing the things
we don't say enough,

words we always
meant to say
but somehow never did.

Words like,

You're amazing!

Just the thought of you

makes me smile.

I'm here if you need me;

I'm so sorry for your loss;

and

You'll always be in my prayers.

What if it became a holiday...

The First Ever Too Seldom Said Day!

Everyone would gather

on brightly lit stages,

or people would write down
on small slips of paper

those unsaid words

of gratitude and praise,

forgiveness or apology,

all long overdue

yet left silently unsaid.

Imagine that day,
when one by one
we waited in our seats

to step out on the stage
and share from the heart,

and finally

my turn came.

I would search
through the audience
for the faces I knew,

and I would speak as if
each were the only one there.

Thank you for the book you lent—

the one I never have returned.

I'm sorry I snapped at you;

I hope you'll forgive me.

Have I ever told you

that you're my hero?

And then I would see you sitting there,
your face a face I cherish.

I would silently say a prayer of thanks
for all you mean to me, and then
I'd read aloud from my little slip of paper:

Too Seldom Said Day

What on earth
could I ever have
done to deserve
such a wonderful
you in my life?
You are a gift
from God!

Those are my words for you today,
my words too seldom said...